Spotted!

by Catherine
Illustrated by S

Contents

Be in Roy Robot's Squad 2
Begin the Quest 3
What Roy Robot Found Out 23
Look It Up and Index 24

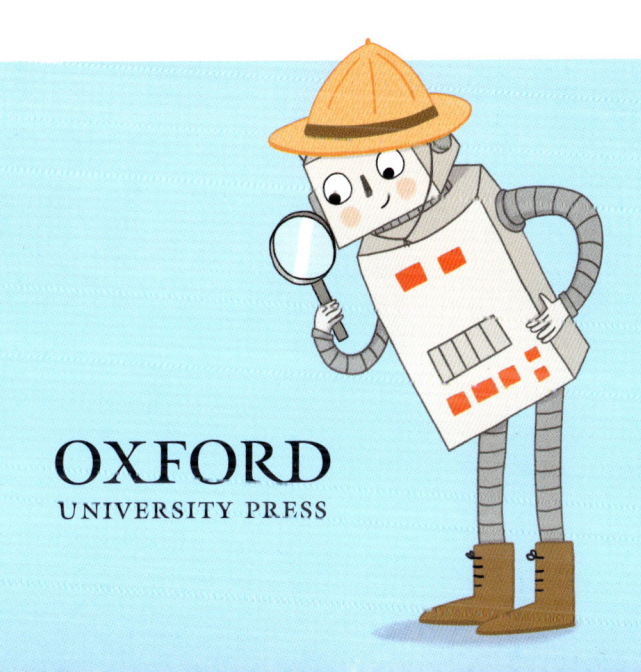

OXFORD
UNIVERSITY PRESS

Be in Roy Robot's Squad

Help Roy Robot on his **quest** to find spots in the wild.

Begin the Quest

Roy is looking for things with spots. He has found this little bug! Its spots mean 'don't eat me'.

I taste awful!

Roy could not miss this bright flower!

Create means to make something new. Roy is creating a drawing of the flower. What sort of pictures do you like to create?

Roy shrieks when he sees the big spots on this bug's wings.

It looked at me!

The bird on this branch is showing off its bright feathers and spots.

I'm behind you, Roy!

Look what Roy has found growing in the shade. Don't eat it, as it could make you sick.

yellow spots

The spots help this hunter to hide as it creeps up on a shield bug.

spider

shield bug

Can you copy the spider's <u>actions</u> and pretend you are creeping up on a bug?

Spots make these flowers look good! Lots of people grow these spotty flowers in their gardens.

If lots of people grow these flowers, does that mean that the flowers are popular or not? Can you think of any other popular plants people grow?

Roy squats in the grass to get a closer look at this moth. Its spots tell its enemies not to eat it.

Don't squash me!

Roy has put on a diving mask to swim in the sea. He has found this spotted thing!

I'm a red starfish!

Look at what Roy has found next!
These fish have white spots all over them.

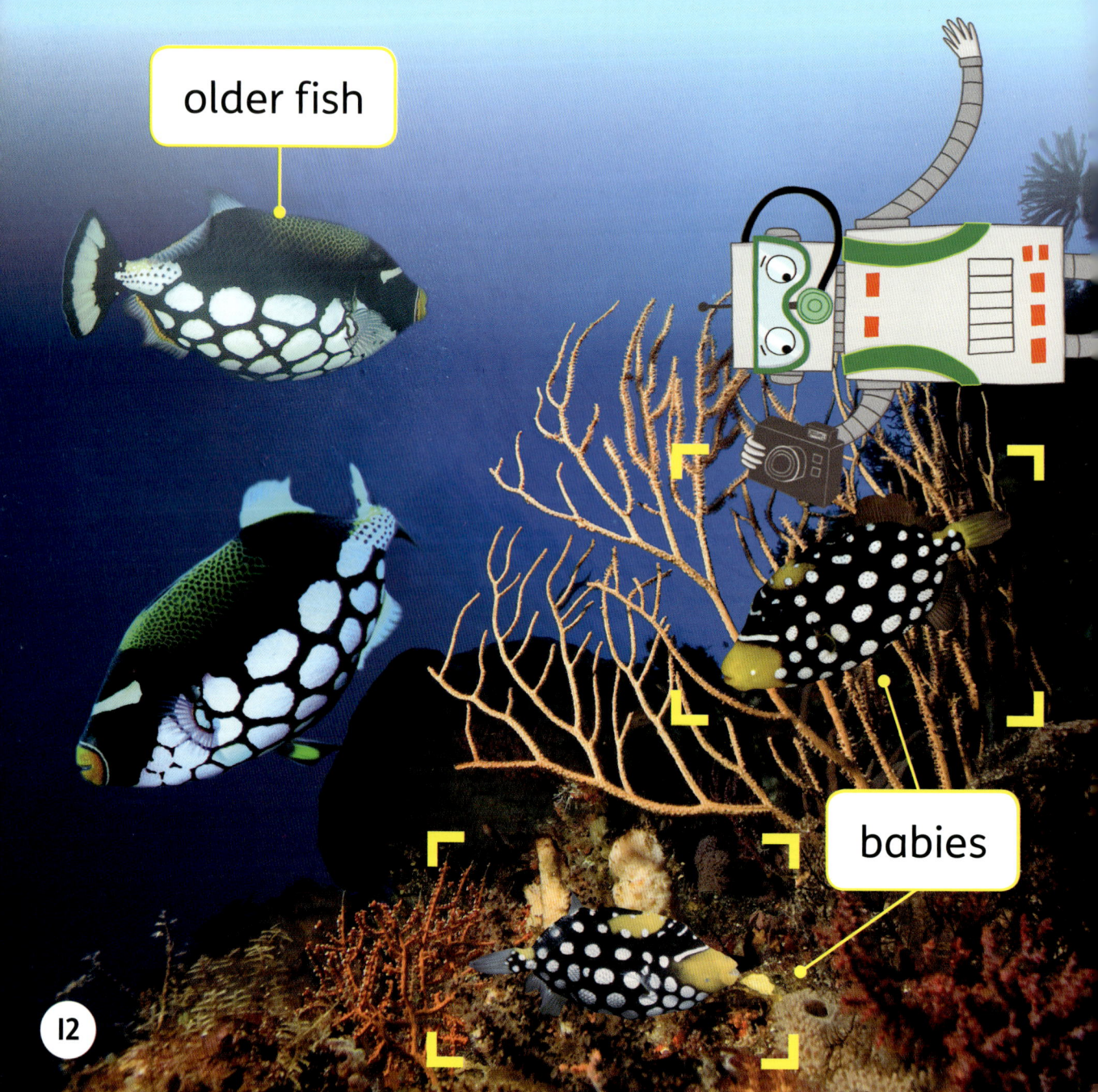

older fish

babies

These **timid** crabs hide inside the **coral** reef.

The reef <u>contains</u> lots of crabs.

crab

Look at the picture. What other creatures does the coral reef <u>contain</u>?

13

The spots on this stingray tell enemies to keep away. Yet cleaner fish can get close to clean it!

stingray

cleaner fish

14

This eel is long and thin like a snake. It hides in narrow holes in the rock.

I am hard to see!

When this octopus is afraid, blue circles show on its skin. Back away fast, as it can kill.

Back on land, Roy is looking at these playful cubs. They were hard to spot at first.

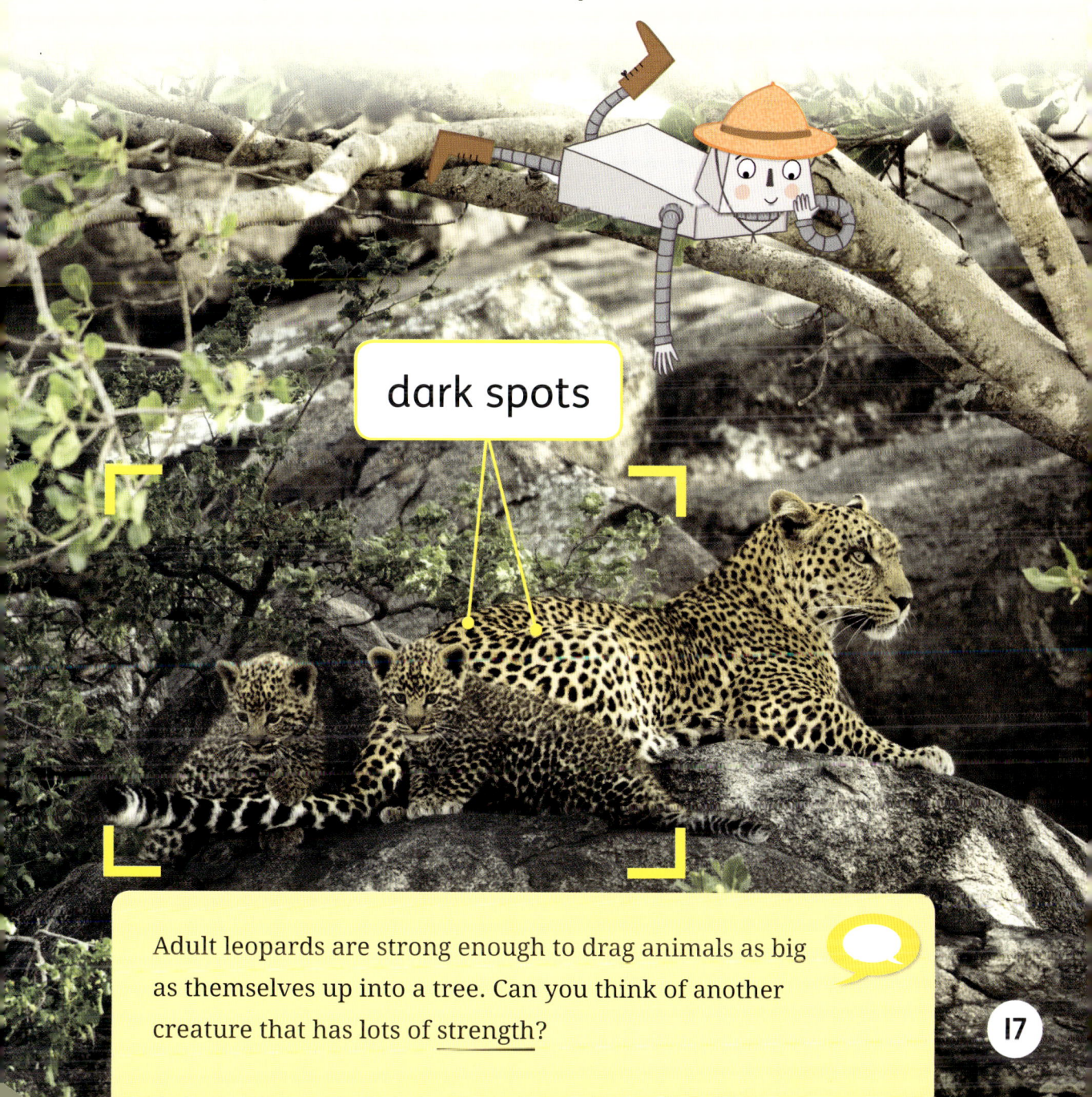

dark spots

Adult leopards are strong enough to drag animals as big as themselves up into a tree. Can you think of another creature that has lots of strength?

The pattern of spots makes this animal hard to see.

This **herd** keeps together to be safe.
The babies are called fawns.

fawns

Deer are nervous animals – they are very easy to scare.
What sorts of things might make them nervous?

19

The spots on this plant show us that it is **toxic**.

toxic leaf

Look out! This frog can kill ten grown men.

Don't rub or eat me!

Oh dear, now I have spots! I need a wash!

What Roy Robot Found Out

In the wild, spots can mean different things.

They can mean *keep away*.

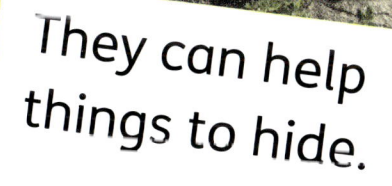

They can mean *look at me*.

They can help things to hide.

Look It Up

coral: animals that look a bit like rocks or plants in the sea
herd: a group of animals
quest: a trip to find things
timid: afraid of lots of things
toxic: full of poison

Index

animal spots 17, 18, 19, 21
bird spots 6
bug spots 3, 5, 8, 10
plant spots............................... 4, 7, 9, 20
sea spots 11, 12, 13, 14, 15, 16

The Look It Up section is also called a Glossary. You can use it to look up the meanings of words that are in **bold** in this book. The Index will help you find key information.